Walking in on People

WALKING IN
ON PEOPLE

POEMS BY

Melissa Balmain

<small>WINNER OF THE</small> 2013 <small>ABLE MUSE BOOK AWARD</small>

ABLE MUSE PRESS

Able Muse Press

www.ablemusepress.com

Printed in the United States of America

Library of Congress Control Number: 2014931534

ISBN 978-1-927409-29-9 (paperback)
ISBN 978-1-927409-30-5 (digital)

Cover design by Alexander Pepple; with images:
    "Jude Face Covered" by Poetic Spectre Imaging /
    "Stockings" by Larissa H /
    "Atamax Background" by Wojciech Obuchowicz

Book design by Alexander Pepple

Able Muse Press is an imprint of *Able Muse:* A Review of Poetry, Prose & Art—at
www.ablemuse.com

Able Muse Press
467 Saratoga Avenue #602
San Jose, CA 95129

For Bill, Davey and Lily,
without whom this would be a much shorter book

Acknowledgments

I am grateful to the editors of the following journals where many of these poems originally appeared, sometimes in earlier versions.

Able Muse: "Two Julys."

American Arts Quarterly: "A Drinker with a Flask."

Babytalk: "Lullabies for the 21st Century."

Brain, Child: "A Bust."

Bumbershoot: "Déjà Blue."

The Formalist: "Thoughts During a Quiet Car Trip."

Kiss and Part (anthology): "Tale of a Relationship, in Four Parts."

Light Quarterly (now *Light*): "Villain *Elle*," "Her Suit," "Hard-shelled," "Shopper's Life List," "Walking in on People," "Endgame," "Lament," "The Marital Bed," "Altered States," "Fruit Suite," "Genus Envy," "New Parent at a Party," "Epiphany While Reading *People* Magazine," "Fluffy Weighs in on the Baby," "Notes from a Jaded Traveler," "Vanishing Lines," "Egypped," "Fit for Life," "Brooklyn Anthem," "To a Toddler," "Toilet Triolet," "April Fools," "A Mother Answers the Question, 'What Have

You Written Lately?'" "Your Rejection Slip, Annotated," "Barnyard Beefs," "Love Poem," "Excuses," "Nightmare," "Walking in the Woods."

Lighten Up Online: "Enfant Terrible," "Fed Up," "Olympic Goals: Theirs and Mine."

Measure: "Memo to Self, in Bed," "Prayer for a Husband," "Al Gore's Ode on Global Warming."

Mezzo Cammin: "Song of the BraBall," "To Phyllis's Ghost," "Tune for the Prune," some of "Afterwords."

Parody: "The Gen-Y Dude to His Friend with Benefits."

The Rotary Dial: "Bird in the Hand."

The Spectator: "To a Friend Who Asked for One Good Reason to Move to the City," "Hypochondriac's Song," "Open Book."

The Washington Post: "Daredevil," some of "Afterwords."

Thanks also to the organizers of the following contests, in which the corresponding poems placed: "Memo to Self, in Bed," finalist, 2005 Howard Nemerov Sonnet competition; "Prayer for a Husband," finalist, 2008 Howard Nemerov Sonnet competition; "Amid Talk of Studio Layoffs, Donald Duck Pops the Question," winner, New England Shakespeare Festival's 2009 Rubber Ducky Sonnet Contest; "Al Gore's Ode on Global Warming," finalist, 2012 X.J. Kennedy Parody Award; "Daredevil," second place, 2012 Washington Post Style Invitational; "Two Julys," finalist, 2013 Able Muse Write Prize.

And huge, heartfelt gratitude to the friends and mentors who commented on drafts of these poems; to my unpaid-yet-unflagging publicists, Earl Weiner and Gina Ingoglia Weiner; and above all to the amazing Bill FitzPatrick, who continues to read everything I write even though I may never get through his critiques of Neo-Kantian constitutivism.

Foreword

By her own admission—her title halloos it!—Melissa Balmain walks in on people at awkward moments. She catches them not only in bed ("Don't think, while you are holding him, of deadlines,/ of monster Visa bills you haven't paid...") but also in committing such bald and piquantly human acts of ordinary living that we cannot help but horse-shake with recognition. It will not be long into this book of poems before you begin to feel, dear reader, that she has been walking in on you, as you square the shoulders of your own unloveliness (Merrill's phrase) against the airbrushed images in a fashion magazine, place a personal ad, envy friends, mop up after babies, or sing your own hypochondriacal songs.

In "Altered States," a woman envies her friends' baby bumps, and then, when she herself is finally pregnant and showing, covets their now slim and tanned physiques. Envy is a serious foible to be sure, but exposing it needn't be serious. In fact, sometimes the light style is the surest weapon for skewering social misdemeanors (and even the occasional plea-bargained felony). A poet friend of mine once pointed out that one of the weaknesses of contemporary poetry is that it can't tell the difference between serious and comic, and I think he's right. The failings and embarrassments of the physical (that stalwart of classical comedy) have been elevated into a "poetics of the body," while serious moral questions are elided with ironic whimsy. Of course, the true poet can hear notes of absurdity in the tragic *(King Lear),* as well as understand the ways in which laughs must be played for keeps (Juvenal's *Satires*), but she is clear about which is which. The light style, blessedly, can eat its cake and have it too, taking the serious seriously but approaching it with a playful dexterity and wit that short-circuits sentimentality.

Like Shakespeare's fool, Robert Armin (who succeeded the broader comedian Will Kemp), Melissa Balmain is both a rug-puller and a truth-teller. Among the spells in her grimoire of verbal wizardry is the enchanting use of a pun. Wrongly deemed a low form of humor, puns can bring two distinct verbal realms crashing together with great economy and verve, as in "Villain *Elle*" (at once a fashion magazine, a fashionable verse form, and a nemesis) and "Her Suit" (about an admirer of follically bounteous women). Balmain's acute gag reflex—for yuks, not yucks!—places her among the finest writers of light verse: she can Cope as well as Wendy, while her lightly sardonic wit and gimlet-eye (at once tipsy and rapier sharp) Parker next to Dorothy. Indeed, Mrs. Parker would have been very pleased to write "Shopper's Life List," which concludes, "A gross of bras/ A score of scarves / A dozen wallets (black) / Ten cars / Eight dogs / Six cats / Three homes / Two canes / One granite plaque." What's more, Balmain manages a tenderness of feeling that eludes more scabrous satirists. She eyes the domestic with wryness, but also with a deep and sustaining warmth.

Balmain's elegy for the editor John Mella, "Vanishing Lines," reminds us that for many years her poems enlivened the pages of Mella's redoubtable quarterly *Light,* the only magazine of its kind in a sea of self-serious verse. (Balmain—tapped by Mella as his successor—is the current editor of *Light,* now an e-zine.) It was a great pleasure, finding in those sometimes perfect-bound and always perfect issues, her poems rubbing elbows with poems by Tom Disch, Robert Conquest, and A.E. Stallings. Now, here they are all together, and as with these other fine poets, a strain of madcap lunacy at times prevails. Take "A Cut Above":

> I've had my share of growths removed,
> from head to chest to toe—
> alarming bumps and wayward clumps
> that surgeons said must go;
> I've been syringed and sliced and stitched,
> then bandaged, bound and billed.
> I shouldn't whine—all proved benign—
> and yet I'm unfulfilled.

After bemoaning all of her pared-away tissues, the woman finds fulfillment on the day of her C-section, where the child she has given birth to is the "growth" she gets to keep!

A mother's love is a special thing. Balmain writes often about the trials of child rearing, but the nursery-rhyme and lullaby quality of some of these poems has been tweaked for parental consumption, constituting a *Grown-up's Garden of Verses*. Despite the trials of child rearing, Balmain can look on the bright side. Just think of all she might accomplish, if she weren't changing nappies all the time, and yet . . . :

> I'd speak Chinese and know the works of Strauss;
> my yard would not have weeds and gophers in it;
> each morning I would swim, bake bread, squeeze juice;
> I'd make the most of every single minute.
> Thank God I've finally got a good excuse.

Amid the loopy flights of imagination—fantasies about freeing lobsters from their tanks, a game of strip chess, a song devoted to an enormous ball of bras, the interstitial annotation of a rejection slip—there is a clutch of what must, for all of their wryness, be acknowledged as sweetly heartfelt amorous verses. Here is the end of the aptly titled "Love Poem," which begins with a litany of cast-off things:

So if, God help us, we are ever tempted
to ditch our marriage when it's lost its glow,
let's give the thing our finest spit and polish—
and, having learned our lesson, not let go.

A good poem is like a long-suffering spouse. For all our waywardness as readers, beset as we are by distractions and laziness (when we'd rather be watching television or listening to a Saturday matinee broadcast from the Met than reading another slim volume), good poems never lose sight of us, despite our propensity to lose sight of them. So many of the poems in Melissa Balmain's triumphant debut lodge themselves in that Frostian zone where they are hard to get rid of. They recur in the mind in moments of hilarity and pathos, of exaltation and mortification, and they never let us go.

—David Yezzi

Contents

III

IV

V

Walking in on People

I

Villain *Elle*

Whenever I wake up and don't feel well,
I like to read a women's magazine.
I know that I can count on *Vogue* or *Elle,*

Cosmo or *Glamour, Self* or *Mademoiselle,*
instead of pills, elixirs or caffeine,
whenever I wake up and don't feel well.

Page Eight has bathing suits that look just swell
if you're six foot and live on Lean Cuisine.
I know that I can count on *Vogue* or *Elle.*

Page Nine's a list of "wardrobe musts" that sell
at reasonable prices—for a queen.
Whenever I wake up and don't feel well,

Page Ten says how to age, yet stay a belle.
The photo? It's a model of eighteen.
I know that I can count on *Vogue* or *Elle*

to make my time in bed such living hell,
I'm out of there in sixty seconds clean.
Whenever I wake up and don't feel well,
I know that I can count on *Vogue* or *Elle.*

Her Suit

Seeking Hairy Woman—This single white
male—42-year-old, handsome professional,
financially secure, well-traveled, who enjoys
the best that life has to offer—seeks a single
female, 30s-40s, who is natural-looking, with
extensive body hair.
— *New York Magazine*

Dear Seeking,

Mama always said
I'd have my pick of guys:
surely someone Euro-bred
would love my hairy thighs,
my hairy breasts, my hairy feet—
such a fluffy pair! —
my hairy stomach (so petite!),
my hairy derrière.

Mama lied. I dated men
with names like Jacques and Ruud,
Antonio and Horst and Sven,
but, once they saw me nude,
they'd act like any Tom or Dave,
mumbling at the floor
about how I could use a shave—
then run right out the door.

I tried all kinds of razor blades;
my coat kept getting thicker.
I waxed, I tweezed, I used pomades;
it sprouted even quicker.
Desperate for a man to kiss,
I splurged on something drastic:
a week of electrolysis
and being wrapped in plastic.

The eighth day, all my hair grew back.
I drank a lot of beer.
Then, at the bar, a guy named Jack
murmured in my ear
he'd caught a glimpse of furry shin
that really turned him on.
At last—a man who liked me in
my bod. We talked past dawn.

Jack had dimples, Jack had charm.
I thought I'd found The One.
He took me to his family's farm;
we always had our fun
in stalls atop a bale or two.
I did enjoy the sex,
until the day we heard a moo,
and Jack sighed, "That's my ex."

Since then I've just been celibate—
it's really not so bad.
But give me, for the hell of it,
what isn't in your ad:
an honest explanation why
you like your women hairy.
And if it sounds convincing, I
might even meet you—

            Wary

Hard-shelled

A noble urge to liberate the lobsters
came over me in Wal-Mart yesterday.
Like stoolies left for dead by Jersey mobsters,
they lay, bound up, inside their little bay.
I thought I'd buy all twenty (how romantic!),
chauffeur them right away to sandy ground,
and watch them scuttle into the Atlantic.
But then I saw they cost ten bucks a pound.

Two hundred dollars just to save crustaceans?
That's my per-annum budget for CDs,
my limit on new Christmas decorations,
my cap for Turkish figs and Gallic cheese.
One lobster waved a feeler—I ignored it.
I'll be a hero when I can afford it.

Shopper's Life List

Nine thousand quarts of orange juice
Five thousand loaves of bread
Eight hundred fifty bars of soap
Three hundred lipsticks (red)
A gross of bras
A score of scarves
A dozen wallets (black)
Ten cars
Eight dogs
Six cats
Three homes
Two canes
One granite plaque

Walking in on People

It's just a talent that I've always had—
though not, thank God, around my mom and dad.
They did the deed; as living proof, I knew it.
And yet I somehow never saw them do it.
The same cannot be said, regrettably,
of roommates, colleagues, hosts and two or three
romantic pairs whose panting thrusts and reaches
were glimpsed by me on isolated beaches;
of poets who—shared sitting rooms be damned—
I witnessed at a conference, enjambed;
of friends rebounding from a recent breakup;
and, once, two mimes in nothing but their makeup.
(They goggled up at me with mute surprise,
their mouths dramatic O's that matched their eyes,
his hand suspended in midair to pet her.
Marcel Marceau could not have done it better.)

Why me? Why all this unintended shock?
I wish I knew—I don't forget to knock,
I never tiptoe like a ballerina,
and still I'm like some Peeping Thomasina.
My consolation is I get for free
a version of what some folks pay to see:
instead of porno actors *in flagrante,*
I'm bound to catch a glimpse of someone's auntie—
and though it will humiliate us both,
while prompting an unconscionable oath
from Uncle Irving, Archibald or Maury,
it's guaranteed to make a better story.

Tale of a Relationship, in Four Parts

Kissing.
Hissing.
Dissing.
Missing.

The Gen-Y Dude to His Friend with Benefits

— Apologies to Marlowe

Come hang with me and all my bros—
we'll grab some brews and Domino's,
and Netflix *The Avengers* next.
Later, maybe we can sext.

Ping me and I will ping you back
a link to my IKEA hack;
to really show I give a damn,
I'll even send an Instagram.

What if I get a sweet Evite
to party down on Friday night?
Then you, my bangable plus-one,
can watch me playing Temple Run

on my new Android while we eat.
Next day, I'll write an awesome tweet
about how you and I should chill
with Jason, Justin, Josh and Bill.

We'll keep this up a month or two,
and then, the way girls always do,
you'll want that *word*. I'll say I've said it
by sharing clips I find on Reddit,

pretending like I'm all engrossed
in random Facebook crap you post,
installing Minecraft on your Dell,
and texting "Sup?" and "LOL."

But no . . . you'll say I'm just a stupid
jerk you met on OkCupid,
and dump my ass. That's how it goes.
I'll keep on hanging with my bros.

Bird in the Hand

It doesn't caw or hunt or fly.
It can't peck anybody's eye
or even grow a single lousy feather.
One-clawed, no match for any tom,
it's stranded on a leafless palm,
regardless of the season, time or weather.

Yet what's the bird that, all alone,
sticks up for you when gibes have flown
and you don't care to verbalize or linger;
when someone's mocked you to your face
or cut you off or swiped your space—
what bird? The one that moonlights as a finger.

Afterwords

Wordsworth

It is a beauteous evening, calm and free.
Let's veg, and watch reality TV.

Bradstreet

Thou ill-formed offspring of my feeble brain,
Thou Twitter tweet, thou make'st me look insane.

Dickinson

A narrow Fellow in the Grass
Took iPhone Pictures of my Ass.

Endgame

"I know," you said, "let's play strip chess!"
It struck me as a winning combo:
nerdy but sexy, like a mambo
done in a Girl Scout leader's dress.

You took two pawns and then my shoes;
a skirt and blouse for both my knights.
A rook, my bra; my queen, my tights.
How ruthlessly you made me lose.

After that you couldn't wait
to pounce, so amorous, so smug,
so clothed. But I escaped your hug
and—sorry, babe—you missed the mate.

Lament

Mama never horsewhipped me
or shoved things up my fanny.
She wasn't hooked on PCP
and didn't bump off Granny.
Daddy never climbed in bed
to open my pajamas.
He read me *Charlotte's Web* instead;
the bed he shared was Mama's.
In college, I did not turn tricks
or date warped literati.
I haven't starved myself to sticks,
joined cults or loved John Gotti.
The guy I married doesn't drink,
or French-kiss other fellers.
It really makes me sad to think
I'll never write best sellers.

II

The Marital Bed

You always hog the blankets
and steal my magazines.
No need to ask what smells so rank—
it's you, the king of beans.

Your toenails cut my shin.
You blow your nose: I jump.
I'm sanded by your bristly chin,
then bulldozed by your rump.

You scratch your back and sigh,
you grunt, harrumph and bray.
And yet the crazy truth is I
can't sleep when you're away.

Fruit Suite

Banana

Bananas are clannish, bananas are true—
an interdependent and unified crew.
One day they're all greenish and hard as bamboo;
the next, they conspire to rot through and through.
So if a well-ripened banana's for you,
then keep the thing lonely, whatever you do.

Peach

Go on: buy one that's dense and round,
that costs two-ninety-nine a pound,
that's fragrant, soft and ruddy gold,
that has no bruises, bugs or mold,
that grew high up a Georgian tree
hand-raised by monks, organically,
with prayer instead of pesticide—
you *still* can't count on juice inside.

Grape

Party eyeball,
Chavez cause,
Bacchan headgear,
sire of laws,
Napa's bounty,
ancient dye,
still-life staple,
bargain buy,
trope for Aesop,
Gallic best,
Welch's cash cow,
Mae's behest,
Kool-Aid flavor,
chore for feet,
and, quite often,
good to eat.

Altered States

I

Everyone seems to be pregnant:
friends of mine, enemies, too.
Women of fifty seem pregnant;
even their husbands look due.

Silences? Pauses? So pregnant.
Ditto each hillside I see.
The whole goddamned planet seems pregnant—
when will it happen to me?

II

And then the stick turns blue at last.
But where are all the taunts I passed?
The pregnant hills? The pregnant folk?
They've disappeared like so much smoke.

Instead I'm in a barren land
where everyone is thin and tanned.
They scrutinize my swollen gut
as if it came from Pizza Hut.

Genus Envy

How nice to be a kangaroo.
Her joey—bald, and slick with goo,
and smaller than a peanut chew—
slips out and climbs inside her pouch;
she doesn't say so much as ouch.
Neither does the average goose.
Without a pause, her egg slides loose,
a nearly frictionless papoose.
Then all she's got to do is nest.
What creature couldn't use the rest?
Maybe not the sterlet fish:
she dumps her brood with one firm swish.
It's true some find them quite delish—
but still, as birthing matters go,
she has an easy roe to hoe.

Such is life for almost all
the mothers on this great blue ball,
those who swim or fly or crawl—
except, of course, the human kind.
Couldn't we be redesigned?

New Parent at a Party

I am sure it's great weed,
   but I don't want a toke.
      It could never be potent enough.
And the same goes for speed,
   LSD, 'shrooms and coke,
      Johnnie Walker, espresso and snuff.

What I long for instead
   is a drug you can't score
      by the gram or the pint or the lid.
All you need is a bed
   and eight hours or more,
      no distractions, no noise and no kid.

To a Friend Who Asked
for One Good Reason
to Move to the City

Let's say you're in the countryside
and craving mocha chip.
It's 3 a.m., too late to ride
to Podunk's tiny strip
of stores (they're closed) and buy a quart.
You'll make your own, you vow.
But there's no milk! So you exhort
your soundly sleeping cow
to give you some; she kicks your shin;
you yelp and wake the horse,
who wakes the pigs and geese, whose din
wakes up your wife, of course.
You trail her, sulking, back to bed—
a hungry man apart.

Let's say you lived in town instead:
you'd hit the Jiffy Mart.

Enfant Terrible

There's a truth that most people prefer to keep quiet,
unshared with their friends and their kin—
but it's high time that everyone ceased to deny it:
a newborn is ugly as sin.
You can dress it in taffeta, ribbon and lace;
you can scrub it each hour of the day;
you can name it Belinda Veronica Grace;
it'll still look like rump roast *manqué.*
Any puppy or kitten is sweeter by far,
any lamb, piglet, gosling or foal—
even marmoset infants make ours seem subpar—
so if having a baby's your goal,
don't expect me to call the thing "darling" or "cutie"
or "precious" or "dear little elf."
Only *one* child has ever been born a real beauty:
the one I gave birth to myself.

Epiphany While Reading *People* Magazine

— Apologies to Franklin P. Adams

If I could trade the things I own
for all the stuff you've got—
the gabled mansion on the Rhône,
the fifty-nine-foot yacht,
the gardens, pools and tennis courts,
the Prada evening dress,
the chef who makes you salmon tortes—
would I find happiness?

Would I be glad to leave the house
that's kept me snug for years;
to lose the shrubs I've pruned, the blouse
I found half-priced at Sears?
Would I be gleeful as I fled
my friendly neighborhood
to join the upper crust instead?
You bet your ass I would.

Song of the BraBall

> From Valley to shining Bay, women are . . . making
> a gesture of liberation: they're sending the bras they
> hate most to El Cerrito artist Emily Duffy. . . . 6,800
> bras [have been] rolled into the BraBall, a 700-pound,
> 43-inch-diameter brassiere-sphere now growing in
> Duffy's garage.
>
> — *The Oakland Tribune*

Sayonara, you Miracle Bras—
we are sick of miraculous itch.
Adios, you maternity bras
with the clasps that make nursing a bitch.
See ya later, you Cross Your Heart Bras
that deprive us of air as we talk,
and you "ultra-strong, never-quit" bras
that collapse while we jog, bike or walk.

Now it's off to the BraBall you go.
We are sorry we wasted our dough,
but at least you can be in a show.
(Any boyfriend or spouse who dares mock
our obsession with lingerie schlock
needs a day in an underwire jock.)

Women used to set fire to their bras—
good for them, not so good for the air.
Now a sculpture constructed of bras
seems just right for the eco-aware.
And besides, it's a hoot that you bras,
with no hooters inside you to tame,
are becoming celebrity bras.
Thanks to you, we've got jiggle-free fame.

What comes next? How will all of this end?
If we're lucky, we'll see a new trend.
Some exhibits we gals recommend:
balls of pumps that have tortured our toes,
balls of shoulder pads, thongs—and who knows?—
we could fill up the Met with our hose.

Fluffy Weighs in on the Baby

It's hairless as an egg—
why bother petting that?
It doesn't purr or groom your leg,
and yet you feed the brat.

Instead of catching mice,
it grapples with its socks.
It's never taken my advice
to use the litter box.

It can't climb up a tree,
it can't chase balls of string,
it leaves you *zero* time for me—
just eat the wretched thing.

III

Notes from a Jaded Traveler

I dreamed I went to Heaven—
it wasn't all that great.
The angel choir was tone deaf;
its harps were second rate.
St. Pete was glumly scrubbing
the bird shit off one gate.

I dreamed I went to Hell next—
it wasn't all that grim.
I'd felt worse heat in Brooklyn,
worse torture at the gym;
Satan and his minions
were belting out a hymn.

I dreamed that neither visit
surprised me much—oh sure,
the Bible promised plenty
that wasn't on my tour,
but what location ever
lives up to its brochure?

A Drinker with a Flask

— After a painting by Théodor Rombouts, 1597-1637

At first blush, you're a party boy fresh from a night
of carousing with corseted wenches—
in the watery light, your expression is bright
as you raise up the tipple that quenches.
But a closer inspection reveals that your chin
has been shaven of stubble this morning,
and it seems that your grin may be starting to thin
after many a minute adorning
a face that—it's clearer now—isn't so young;
and your biceps have probably tired
as the bottle, sans bung, has just hung there, and hung. . . .
Yes, your zeal for this scene has expired.
Still, the painter's your friend—or is willing to pay
you to pose—and the booze smells sublime,
so you've promised to stay, feigning fervor all day,
the Heineken man of your time.

Vanishing Lines

— For John Mella, 1941-2012

Although, with age, most men turn denser,
you never flubbed a word of Spenser;

you quoted Coleridge in full voice,
along with Tennyson and Joyce,

then effortlessly rattled off
some Aiken, Shakespeare, Nabokov,

Yeats, Milton, Wodehouse, Hardy, Donne,
Pope, Wordsworth, Hopkins, Dickinson,

Nash, Browning, Keats and Disch to us,
and, in between, Anonymous;

in rumbles ever sure and rich,
you knew to vary pace and pitch

and match selections to events,
the seasons and your audience,

from winter storm to summer wedding,
to women you had hopes of bedding.

But now—we simply can't ignore it—
you've stopped and we are poorer for it.

What happened to your Blake? Your Poe?
Where are your words? Where did they go?

Tune for the Prune

I wish they'd leave your name alone—
so spare and saturnine in tone,
the perfect word for kids to groan
each time that Grandma stews you.
But no: the grocers have to come
and change your label to "dried plum"
in hopes, I guess, they'll make some dumb
gourmets decide to choose you.

What's next? The raisin will be gone
once "dried grape" joins the lexicon—
and then the trend will carry on,
from house to street to diner,
as arbiters of taste and tact
get wind of this renaming act
and seize the moment to redact
some terms they wish were finer.

Although at first they'll stick with food,
rechristening to suit the mood
of those who find plain menus rude,
they'll soon march past the larder.
No word of any kind will be
exempt from *faux* gentility:
instead of death, we'll have "dried chi";
instead of hate, "dried ardor."

Poor prune, of course you had no clue
they'd make a precedent of you,
but quickly now, before they do,
please grant me one small favor:
from wizened skin to rocky pit,
don't be the latest upscale hit.
A change of name can't change a bit
of your repulsive flavor.

Fit for Life

They warn the transformation's subtle:
your boobs will droop, and then your butt'll,
and all the rest that's blessed about you—
tight abs, trim thighs, the bee-stung pout you
    prize—won't last, and that's the truth.

But what you never hear them mention
is how your flair for condescension
to tighter, trimmer, younger women—
"Just watch that bimbo reeling *him* in"—
    will never lose the bloom of youth.

Fed Up

Red Riding Hood's grandma had chest pains galore,
cholesterol looming at two-forty-four,
and blood-pressure spikes. Though she kept it all quiet,
her daughter found out and imposed a strict diet.
No more would she bundle Red off with a pail
of cookies for Granny; instead she sent kale
and casseroles ranging from foul to insipid
because she had stripped them of every known lipid.
One day Red arrived to find Granny in bed.
"Come closer, my dumpling," the dowager said.
Forget the lame cover-up tale that came later:
No wolf gobbled Red. It was Granny who ate her.

Brooklyn Anthem

— To the tune of "America the Beautiful"

O beautiful for pizza pies,
Falafel and knishes.
(Who cares if turf wars send some guys
To sleep among the fishes?)
Buh-ROOK-a-lyn, Buh-ROOK-a-lyn,
A tasty melting pot!
(Just pick a good, safe neighborhood
Where you will not get shot.)

O beautiful for gentrified
Row houses and chai lattes.
(Ignore the bistros full of snide
Celebs who do Pilates.)
Buh-ROOK-a-lyn, Buh-ROOK-a-lyn,
A place of rising means!
(The multitudes who cook its foods
Are moving out to Queens.)

Memo to Self, in Bed

Don't think, while you are holding him, of deadlines,
of monster Visa bills you haven't paid,
of NPR reports on gangs and breadlines
and kooks with nukes available for trade.

Don't think of whom you owe a three-course dinner,
of editors you wish you had impressed,
of whether you should be two sizes thinner
and twice as nice to look at when undressed.

Above all, never think of how time's racing
toward commonplaces you're afraid to name—
white halls, bleak calls, the foregone mortal ending;

how you or he (which one?) will soon be facing
long nights where solitaire's the only game.
Don't think: just wink at him and keep pretending.

Daredevil

— In memory of *Jackass* star Ryan Dunn

When it came to wild stunts, he was second to none—
so who'd have predicted that Ryan M. Dunn
would die, not by catapult, cannon or cougar,
or Russian roulette with a dung-coated Luger,
or by tying himself to a runaway moose,
or snorting ground glass off a lion's caboose,
but by drinking and driving? How could he succumb
to an impulse so achingly, *commonly* dumb?

Afterwords

Burns

O My Luve's like a red, red rose.
He should've put more sunblock on his nose.

Wordsworth

A host of golden daffodils
Gave me rhinitis. I took pills.

Keats

When I have fears that I may cease to be
I get my sperm stored cryogenically.

Egypped

They saved their gold and jewels to buy
the finest in sarcophagi
and scrolls describing how they planned
to live forever in a land
of peace and dainty dishes.

Now in a gallery they lie
where hordes from Flatbush—never shy—
compete to gobble all the canned
historic info they can stand,
then chase it with knishes.

Hypochondriac's Song

Whenever thoughts of dying bring me low,
I tell myself, at least by then I'll know
which trauma or disease has killed me by degrees,
or clobbered me with one efficient blow.

While croaking, I won't fear that UV rays
or germs on cell phones, door knobs and filets,
or poisons leached from soils, or saturated oils,
could spell a tragic ending to my days;

magnetic fields, asbestos, deer ticks, gin,
mad cow disease, lead paint and saccharin
won't fill me with alarm—for what can do me harm
if I've been irreversibly done in?

Just one last thing will smother me with dread:
the notion of the nothingness ahead.
But that will vanish, too, the moment that I'm through—
a perk, I must admit, of being dead.

IV

Lullabies for the 21st Century

Twinkle, twinkle, cutie-poo,
Preschool apps will soon be due.
Though you're only nine months old,
It's tot-eat-tot, so I've been told.
Time to bribe a board or two—
Preschool apps will soon be due.

Hush, little baby, don't say a word,
Mama's gonna buy you a talking bird.
And when its microchip breaks down,
Mama's gonna buy you a dancing clown.
And when it gets recalled next week,
Mama's gonna buy you some mice that squeak.
And when they all get vacuumed up,
Mama's gonna buy you a singing pup.
And when it wastes twelve batteries,
Mama's gonna buy you some plastic keys.
And when they snap in just one day,
Mama's gonna put her purse away.

Lullaby, and good night,
But first answer this right:
What's the square root of four
And the French word for "door"?
Very good—you've worked hard!
Have a new "genius" card!
Lay you down now, and rest,
So you'll pass your next test.

Trans fats are bad, dilly dilly,
Sugar is, too.
I can't buy food willy-nilly,
Now I have you.
What's in this canned chili chili?
What's in this stew?
My eyes are crossed silly silly,
Shopping for you.

To a Toddler

If you were less demanding, I'd write novels;
I'd paint and sew and keep a spotless house;
my deeds would be as bold as Vaclav Havel's;
I'd speak Chinese and know the works of Strauss;
my yard would not have weeds and gophers in it;
each morning I would swim, bake bread, squeeze juice;
I'd make the most of every single minute.
Thank God I've finally got a good excuse.

To Phyllis's Ghost

As a special bonus, a number of the author's cherished
and proven recipes are included.

— From the flyleaf of *Sixpence in Her Shoe*
by Phyllis McGinley

It certainly is wonderful to learn
the secrets of your silky hollandaise,
your sauerbraten no gourmet would spurn,
your super dumplings, pies and *sauce béarnaise.*
(How full your family must have been, most days.)
But still—I hope my tastes won't seem too odd—
there's just one question I would like to raise:
What was the recipe for your ballade?

This is no passing, trivial concern:
I need it—plus your tips on triolets,
sonnets and epigrams. (Mine often burn
like unwatched beans, or sag like failed soufflés.)
Please tell me how to boil down a phrase
and tenderize my meter, tough as sod,
to satisfy a reader's hungry gaze.
Reveal the recipe for your ballade.

Let's face it now, before we must adjourn:
although you may have rolled great canapés,
then browned them to a perfect crispy turn,
the reason you won half the nation's praise
was not your richly laden hostess trays.
How can it be, in all the years you trod,
you shared advice on how to bake and braise,
but not the recipe for your ballade?

Phyllis, I'm betting that these selfish ways
have landed you a little far from God.
So, quick, if you've grown weary of the blaze:
What was the recipe for your ballade?

Toilet Triolet

OK, let's go! It's time to use the potty!
No way you're wearing diapers from now on.
Excuse me, there's no need to act so snotty—
OK? Let's go. It's time to use the potty.
Wait, put your leg back down! You're not a Scottie!
And aim! No, not at Mommy! At the john!
OK, let's go. It's time to use the potty?
No way. You're wearing diapers from now on.

April Fools

Each year they do the same damn thing:
bulbs bloom and start to glow,
then—whammo! Sayonara, spring!—
a cold snap knocks them low.
You'd think by now they'd finally learn
to wait a week or three
until the risk of freezer burn
is gone, but no siree:
come April, come a hint of sun,
they'll pop back up for sure,
to make it seem that winter's done—
and sucker us once more.

Al Gore's Ode on Global Warming

— Apologies to Wordsworth

I wandered, lonely, through a cloud
Of carbon in the Nashville hills,
When, near a sign (No Dogs Allowed),
I saw a clump of daffodils
As yellow as Velveeta cheese.
I groaned, "It's January. *Please.*"

In February things got worse
As flower after flower bloomed—
Trout lily, toothwort, shepherd's purse.
In March? Cicadas. We were doomed.
None of my trophies made me chipper.
I glumly sunbathed, missing Tipper.

Then—April! My depression passed.
True Spring had come and life was swell;
The air felt seasonal at last.
I took a stroll with my Nobel . . .
Until a blizzard hit. Good Lord.
With climate change you're never bored.

I ran inside to warm back up,
Pulled on my favorite sweater (hemp),
Rocked out to Etheridge, brewed a cup—
And when I reached a comfy temp,
I closed my eyes and walked those hills
Of inconvenient daffodils.

A Cut Above

I've had my share of growths removed,
from head to chest to toe—
alarming bumps and wayward clumps
that surgeons said must go;
I've been syringed and sliced and stitched,
then bandaged, bound and billed.
I shouldn't whine—all proved benign—
and yet I'm unfulfilled.
Instead of making useful parts,
my body (why oh why?)
crafts sorry knots and random clots
I have to kiss goodbye.
But things are looking up at last:
today's C-section day!
I wear a smile as, all the while,
the scalpel slits away;
soon hands reach in to ease you from
your long aquatic sleep;
I hear a shout; you're lifted out—
a growth I get to keep.

A Mother Answers the Question, "What Have You Written Lately?"

I've got a newborn poem.
By night she marks her beat
against the bumpers of her crib
with quick iambic feet.

From neck to hip to ankle,
her pithy lines enjamb,
harmonious in form and tone—
a model epigram.

By day she's all sprung rhythm;
a pen just can't contain
those assonantal squeals and coos,
that boldly burped refrain.

I get her down on paper—
the "ultra-leak-proof" type—
then scan her ending (feminine),
and edit with a wipe.

Your Rejection Slip, Annotated

Dear Writer [*who's not dear and cannot write*],
Thank you for showing us your [*so-called*] work.
[*It's obvious that you're a clueless jerk
and typed the thing while higher than a kite.*]
Although we read [*three words of*] it with care,
we'll have to pass [*a kidney stone or two—
or so it seemed when we were reading you.
We also felt like tearing out our hair*].
Unfortunately [*fortunately*], we
get many [*better*] manuscripts each week
[*spam, takeout menus, notes from creditors*],
so [*if we want to keep our sanity*]
we can't give [*drunks like you*] a full critique.
Good luck [*at Betty Ford*],
                                        The Editors

Barnyard Beefs

Hogs emit at least 160 odorous compounds—trace
amounts of gases that rise off their skin and their
waste. . . . "It stinks about enough to make you sick,"
said Kurt Kelsey, whose family has farmed near Iowa
Falls since 1860.

— *Los Angeles Times*

I: The Farmer's Report

The hogs sure stink. The cattle, too.
The horses? Whoa. The sheep? Pee-ewe.
And for a stench that truly sickens,
go get a lungful by the chickens.

II: The Animals' Retort

You pen us up, you brand our butts,
you dock our beaks, you clip our nuts—
then call us smelly? We ain't thinkers,
but we can name the biggest stinkers.

A Bust

Ice cream made of pasteurised human breast milk? Yes, it's called Baby Gaga and it's sold in central London. . . . The inventor of Baby Gaga, Matt O'Connor, was staggered with the response from the public, who went to eat a dollop of ice cream churned with the milk of Victoria Hiley, a London mother of 35, Madagascan vanilla pods and the zest of a lemon and served with a wafer and a shot of Calpol or Bonjela, for an equally staggering 14 pounds, or 23 USD."

— *Pravda.ru*

What a waste.
Though Matt and Vic
piqued public taste
with one swift lick,
no milk of mine
(sweet, creamy-white,
fresh
day and night)
made foodies pine
to churn it up with fruit and spices, then sell each cup at five-star prices.
Chowhound, Zagat,
the evening news,
ran no reviews.
Instead I sat
for years, ill-lit,
while diners (two)
slurped, wriggled, bit,
burped, scratched and grew.
Fame stayed elusive.
At least,
I vaunt,
no res-
taurant
was more exclusive.

V

Déjà Blue

When leaving for a family trip,
I feel my spirits start to slip
before our plane's ascended;
I see us sunburned, flying back
to clean our house, pay bills, unpack—
the fun already ended.

While watering a perky row
of daisies on my patio,
I dread October's freezes,
and picture every stem turned brown,
each shriveled leafstalk hanging down,
each petal gone to Jesus.

I can't enjoy my toddler's coo
without the thought that soon she's due
for angst and boyfriend trouble;
I can't admire my son's smooth face,
and not foresee a nasty case
of zits and razor stubble.

And yet, whenever I get stuck
in traffic, meetings, roadside muck
or something else unpleasant,
imagination's doors bang shut
and I'm marooned in nothing but
the godforsaken present.

Thoughts During a Quiet Car Trip

In the years when our marriage was peerless and new,
I dismissed people's claims that, one day,
even lovers who chatted as much as we two
would be lovers with little to say.

Now behold—we discuss our week's plans well enough,
and our kids and careers, then turn dull,
having long ago drained our supply of the stuff
we could jabber about in a lull:

Which ten movies or books or CDs would we pack
if we knew we'd be stuck on an isle?
Where'd we most like to live—Santa Fe? Fond du Lac?
Is it true that a dolphin can smile?

And what dishes would each of us hanker to eat
on death row, for our very last meal?
And which day is the one we would want to repeat?
And is parapsychology real?

You've announced whom you'd drink with, if given your pick
from among all the living and dead.
I've declared that I'd rather kiss Bowie than Mick,
but would chew on a sneaker instead.

We've debated religion, the meaning of life,
whether love is a matter of luck,
who was funniest (Gomer? Aunt Bee? Barney Fife?),
how we'd spend fifty mil, to the buck.

So we're left to just sit, yawn and sigh, hum a tune,
like the bulk of paired women and men.
But don't worry: senility's bound to hit soon.
Then we'll say it all over again.

Afterwords

Shakespeare

My mistress' eyes are nothing like the sun—
But wait until her laser treatment's done!

Herrick

Whenas in silks my Julia goes,
My Visa bill just grows and grows.

Wyatt

They flee from me, that sometime did me seek.
My Arrid Extra Dry ran out this week.

Love Poem

The afternoon we left our first apartment,
we scrubbed it down from ceiling to parquet.
Who knew the place could smell like lemon muffins?
It suddenly seemed nuts to move away.

The morning someone bought our station wagon,
it gleamed with wax and every piston purred.
That car looked like a centerfold in *Hot Rod!*
Too late, we saw that selling was absurd.

And then there was the freshly tuned piano
we passed along to neighbors with a wince.
We told ourselves we'd find one even better;
instead we've missed its timbre ever since.

So if, God help us, we are ever tempted
to ditch our marriage when it's lost its glow,
let's give the thing our finest spit and polish—
and, having learned our lesson, not let go.

Amid Talk of Studio Layoffs,
Donald Duck Pops the Question

Daisy, you know I've always worshipped you—
remember how we met in 1940
in "Mr. Duck Steps Out," your big debut?
I'd never seen a chick who looked so sporty
(that brazen bow of yours)! There was more pluck
in every feather of your sexy waddle—
in each webbed toe—than in that wild duck
I danced with at the Drake (a swimsuit model).
And though the decades certainly have flown,
and our careers are dead as Buster Keaton,
my love for you, dear bird, has only grown.
So please say yes—before we're stewed and eaten
by suits who downsize via fricassee.
Let's save our necks with sweet publicity.

Prayer for a Husband

Dear God, I've seen him die a thousand times:
while choking on a sandwich at his desk
(he dials for help, but cannot speak—grotesque),
while making foolishly abstracted climbs
(nose-deep in Socrates, he skips a stair),
while doing 80 on Route 81,
or getting mugged by wackos with a gun,
or jogging past an irritable bear.
These deaths are fictional, admittedly—
mere figments when I'm waiting and he's late,
a worrywart's compulsory ordeal.
But still, I'm optimistic you'll agree,
with all he's suffered in my mind to date,
you needn't bother killing him for real.

Excuses

Facing his final days of life,
a father often wishes
he'd spent more hours with kids and wife—
not washed more dinner dishes.

A dying mother's last regrets?
She should have found more time
to play with family and pets—
not scrubbed more bathtub slime.

And so, in preparation for
a happier demise,
we think it's best if we ignore
the urge to sanitize.

Two Julys

Seven months

By now the fireworks surely have begun,
the music and the battery of cheers—
too bright and loud for your new eyes and ears.
So here I stand, a mile from all the fun:
Your body strapped to mine, as dense as stone,
I scan our patchy lawn. I smell a skunk.
I picture celebrating friends—free, drunk—
then stop and gape at what is ours alone.

Mere feet from us, across the cul-de-sac,
not near the grass the way they've always been,
but high among a neighbor's redbud trees,
salvos of lightning bugs flash gold on black.
You nestle silently beneath my chin
as we drink in the night's festivities.

Seven years

The bugs are putting on a show again:
they glitter in a field of early corn.
We've come here, to the town where you were born,
in answer to your never-ending "When?",
your urgency to play where you once played.
Last night you twirled beneath unbroken sky.
A sparkler burned your thumb; you didn't cry.
You saw and heard the fireworks, unafraid.

Now as the insects loop-the-loop and blink,
you race with friends, too far away for me
to see the game or know if you're unharmed.
Some bugs, though separated, fire in sync—
like us, I tell myself, like family.
I wait beside the cornfield, empty-armed.

Nightmare

Your TV cable's on the fritz.
Your Xbox is corroded.
Your iPod sits in useless bits.
Your Game Boy just imploded.

Your cell phone? Static's off the scale.
Your land line? Disconnected.
You've got no mail—E, junk or snail.
Your hard drive is infected.

So here you idle, dumb and blue,
with children, spouse and mother—
and wish you knew what people do
to entertain each other.

Open Book

Time was, your hands were on me night and day.
(The thrill along my spine!) Of course I flipped
for you, from A to Z and back to A,
not once suspecting our romantic script
was doomed (and how), you fickle, shallow fool.
You've traded everything you shared with me—
defining moments, leisurely, old school—
for quickies with your laptop, your PC,
your iPad, iPhone, iDon't-Give-a-Damn:
amid their breathless litany of news,
blogs, tweets, directions, recipes and spam,
they will, at any moment that you choose,
look up a word (or dozens!) in a flash.
Well, here's a definition I find merry:
Comeuppance *(noun):* when all your gadgets crash,
and you crawl back to me—your dictionary.

Olympic Goals:
Theirs
and Mine

Pole Vaulting

To battle forces massive and inertial.
To leave the couch for snacks at a commercial.

Gymnastics

To stick her dismount from the balance beam.
To glue my molars shut with butter cream.

Beach Volleyball

To show the world that she's a slammin' hottie.
To pound some macadamia biscotti.

Swimming

To win more gold than anybody's won.
To grab that lemon square before my son.

Marathon

To run despite the agony that melts her.
To dash upstairs in search of Alka-Seltzer.

Walking in the Woods

This euphoria's bound to fade quickly—
in a minute or two, maybe less.
I'm on deadline, my husband is prickly,
my garage, house and yard are a mess,
I can't sleep, my investments are reeling,
and I have to go in for a scan;
so this giddy, ridiculous feeling
has been doomed since before it began.
If the oaks weren't so brazenly amber,
if the pines smelled a fraction less sweet,
if that thrush had a mousier timbre,
I'd be moping and dragging my feet.
This euphoria clearly won't make it;
it's a nutty illusion. I'll take it.

MELISSA BALMAIN edits *Light,* an online journal of light verse. Her poems have appeared in such anthologies as *The Iron Book of New Humorous Verse* and *Killer Verse,* and in many American and British journals and magazines. The author of a memoir, *Just Us: Adventures and Travels of a Mother and Daughter,* she has published articles and humor pieces in *The New Yorker, McSweeney's, Success,* and *The New York Times.* She teaches at the University of Rochester and lives nearby with her  husband and two children. *Walking in on People,* the winner of the 2013 Able Muse Book Award, is her first full-length poetry collection. She hopes its title won't discourage people from having her as a houseguest.

OTHER BOOKS FROM ABLE MUSE PRESS

Ben Berman, *Strange Borderlands - Poems*

Michael Cantor, *Life in the Second Circle - Poems*

Catherine Chandler, *Lines of Flight - Poems*

Maryann Corbett, *Credo for the Checkout Line in Winter - Poems*

Margaret Ann Griffiths, *Grasshopper - The Poetry of M A Griffiths*

Ellen Kaufman, *House Music - Poems*

Carol Light, *Heaven from Steam - Poems*

April Lindner, *This Bed Our Bodies Shaped - Poems*

Frank Osen, *Virtue, Big as Sin - Poems*

Alexander Pepple (Editor), *Able Muse Anthology*

Alexander Pepple (Editor), *Able Muse - a review of poetry, prose & art*
   (semiannual issues, Winter 2010 onward)

James Pollock, *Sailing to Babylon - Poems*

Aaron Poochigian, *The Cosmic Purr - Poems*

Stephen Scaer, *Pumpkin Chucking - Poems*

Hollis Seamon, *Corporeality - Stories*

Matthew Buckley Smith, *Dirge for an Imaginary World - Poems*

Barbara Ellen Sorensen, *Compositions of the Dead Playing Flutes - Poems*

Wendy Videlock, *The Dark Gnu and Other Poems*

Wendy Videlock, *Nevertheless - Poems*

Richard Wakefield, *A Vertical Mile - Poems*

www.ablemusepress.com

CPSIA information can be obtained at www.ICGtesting.com
Printed in the USA
LVOW13s1429060714

393058LV00004B/531/P